Will you come to my party?

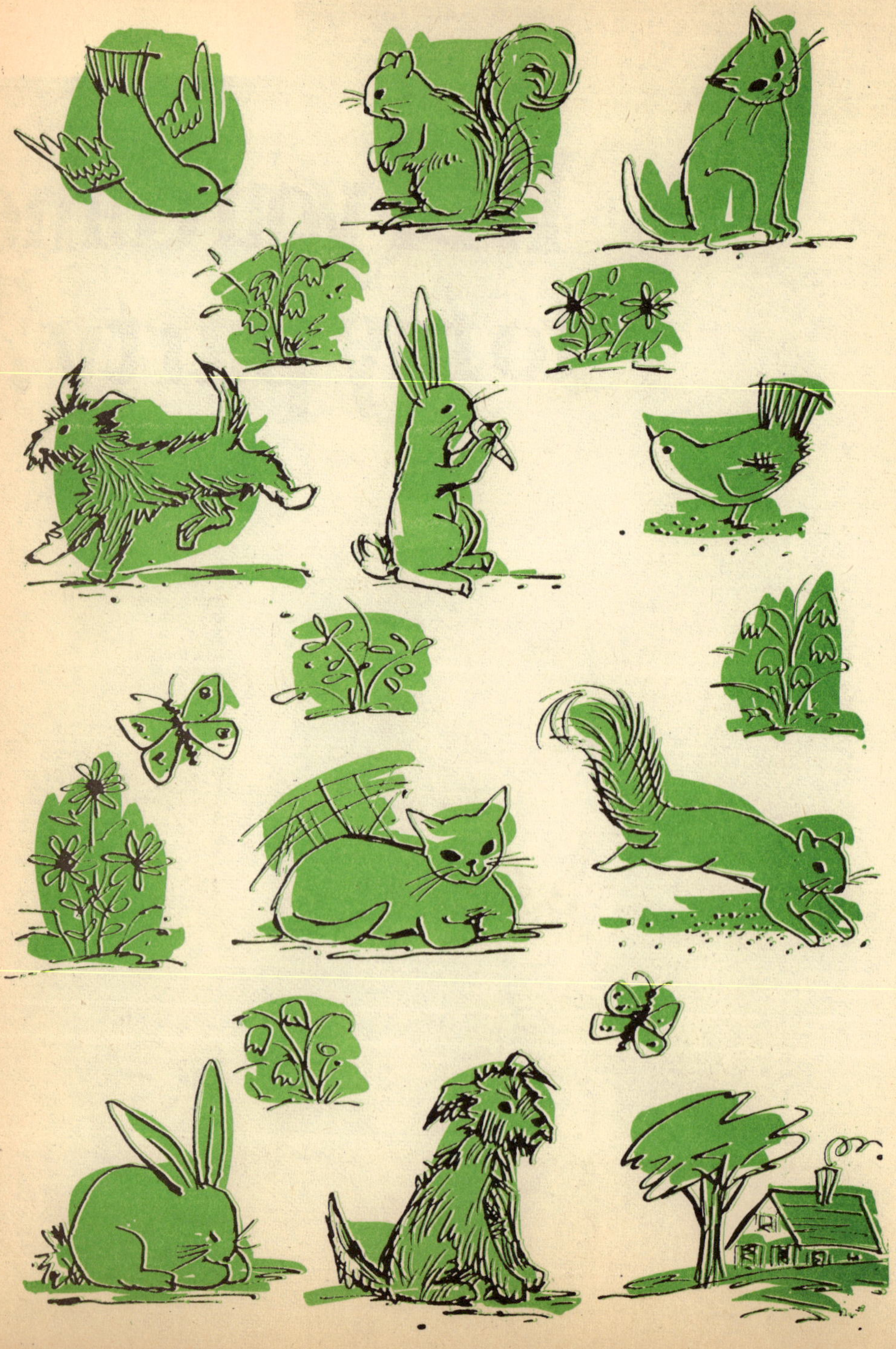

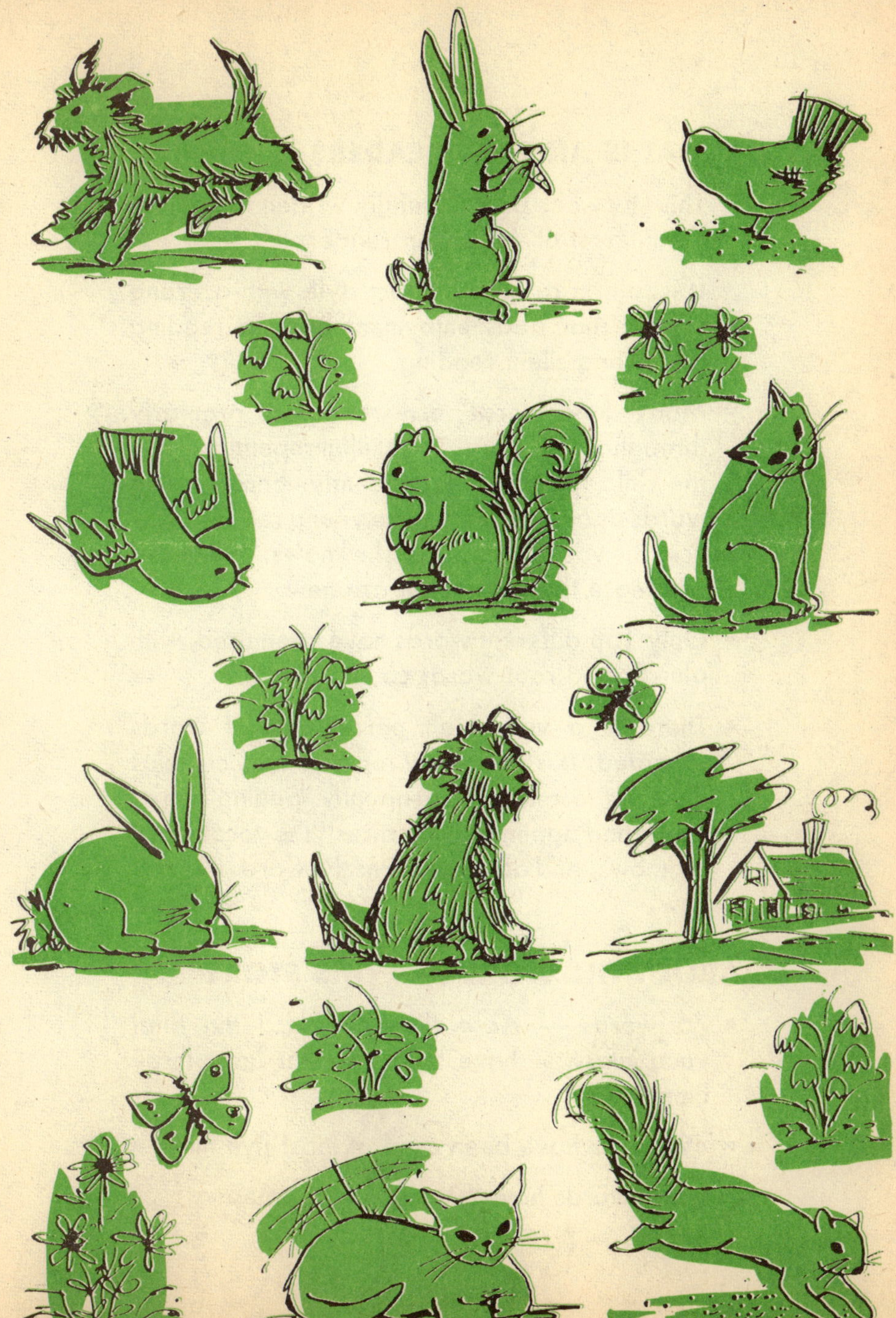

WHAT IS AN EASY READER?

- This story has been carefully written to capture the interest of the young reader.

- It is told in a simple, direct style with a strong rhythm that adds enjoyment both to reading aloud and silent reading.

- Many key words are repeated regularly throughout the story. This skillful repetition helps the child to read independently. Encountering words again and again, the young reader practices the vocabulary he or she knows, and learns with ease the words that are new.

- Only 168 different words have been used, with plurals and root words counted once.

- There is a very high percentage of words repeated. *It is this skillful repetition which helps the child to read independently.* Seeing words again and again, he "practices" the vocabulary he knows, and actually learns the words that are new.

ABOUT THE WORDS IN THIS STORY

- 76 words — *more than one-third the total vocabulary* — have been used at least three times.

- 49 words have been used at least five times.

- Some words have been used 34 times.

Will you come to my party?

Story by SARA ASHERON
Pictures by SUSANNE SUBA
Editorial Consultant
LILIAN MOORE

Wonder® Books
PRICE/STERN/SLOAN
Publishers, Inc., Los Angeles
1986

Introduction

Easy Readers help young readers discover what a delightful experience reading can be. The stories are such fun that they inspire children to try new reading skills. They are so easy to read that they provide encouragement and support for children as readers.

The adult will notice that the sentences aren't too long, the words aren't too hard, and the skillful repetition is like a helping hand. What the child will feel is: "This is a good story—and I can read it myself!"

For some children, the best way to meet these stories may be to hear them read aloud at first. Others, who are better prepared to read on their own, may need a little help in the beginning—help that is best given freely. Youngsters who have more experience in reading alone—whether in first or second or third grade—will have the immediate joy of reading "all by myself."

These books have been planned to help all young readers grow—in their pleasure in books and in their power to read them.

Lilian Moore
Specialist in Reading
Formerly of Division of Instructional Research,
New York City Board of Education

Copyright © 1961, 1981 by Price/Stern/Sloan Publishers, Inc.
Published by Price/Stern/Sloan Publishers, Inc.
410 North La Cienega Boulevard, Los Angeles, California 90048

Printed in the United States of America. All rights reserved. No part of this publication may be reproduced, stored in a retrieval system, or transmitted, in any form or by any means, electronic, mechanical, photocopying, recording, or otherwise, without the prior written permission of the publishers.

ISBN: 0-8431-4305-3

Wonder® Books is a trademark of Price/Stern/Sloan Publishers, Inc.

Little Gray Squirrel looked around.

Where was the little boy?

Where was the little girl?

He ran into the garden.

He looked under the tree.

No boy!

No girl!

There was Old White Cat,
sitting in the sun.
There was Old Brown Dog.

There was little Sparrow Bird,

talking, talking, way up in the tree.

There was Bunny Rabbit, going
hop-hop-hop around the garden.
No boy!
No girl!

"Where is the little boy today?"
asked Little Gray Squirrel.
"And where is the little girl?"

"I know! I know!"
Sparrow called down
from the tree.
"They went to a party."
"A party!" said Little Gray Squirrel
in surprise.
"Is it somebody's birthday?"

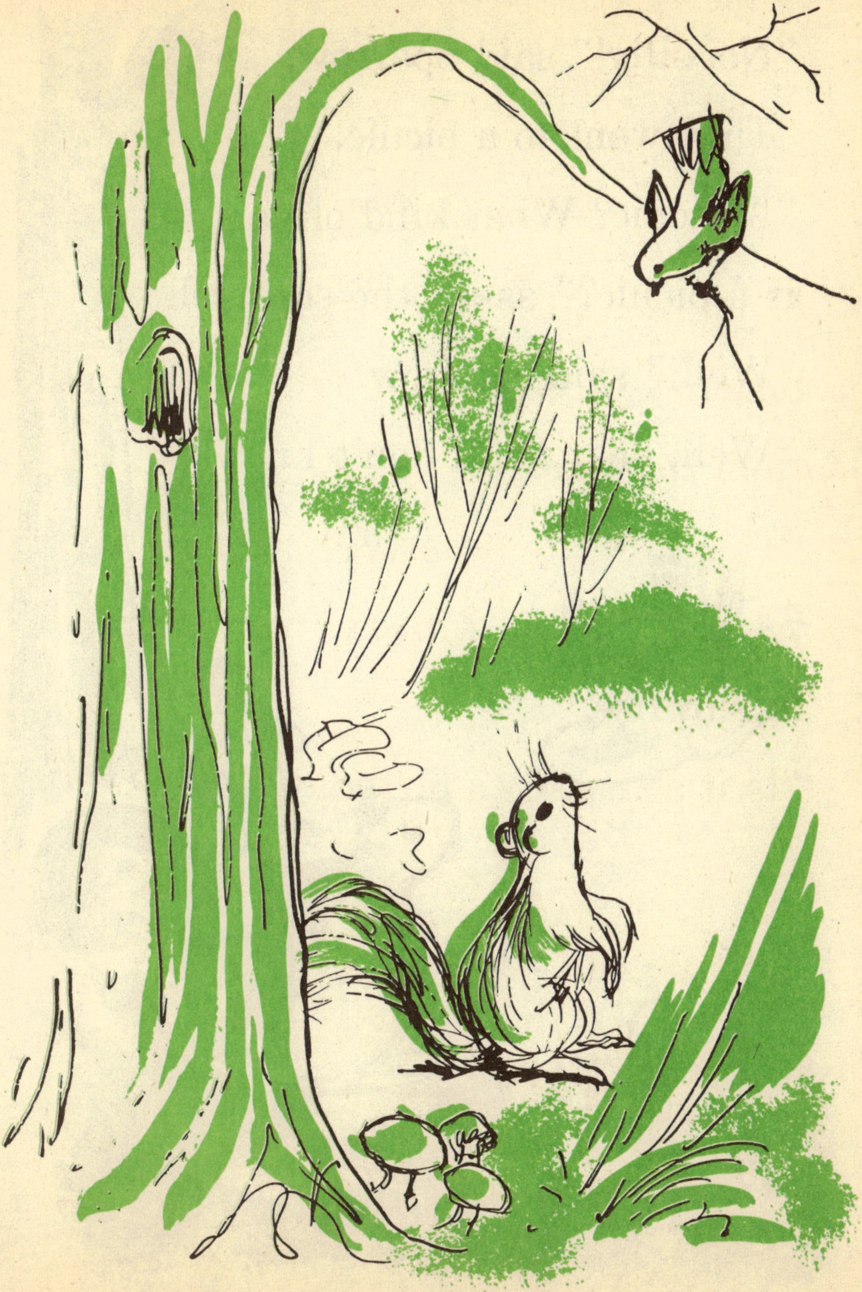

"No, silly!" said Sparrow.

"They went to a picnic."

"A picnic? What kind of party is a picnic?" asked the squirrel.

"Well," said Sparrow.

"Well, dear me! I don't know!"

Old Brown Dog looked up.

"I think it's an eating party,"

he said.

"Everybody eats and eats—

and *eats*."

An eating party!

My, that did sound good!

Little Gray Squirrel ran
all the way home.

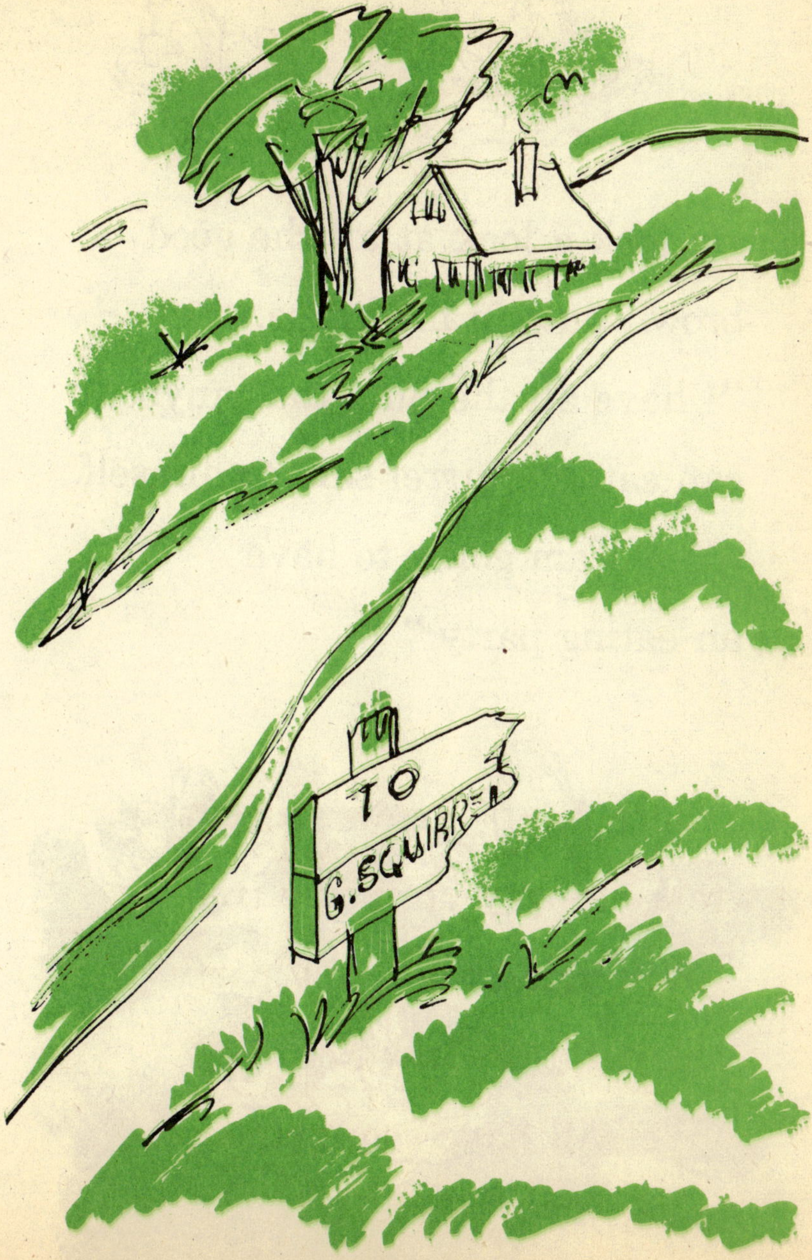
TO
G.SQUIRREL

He took a look at all the good
brown nuts in his house.
"I have all the nuts that anybody
can eat," Squirrel said to himself.
"Yes, I am going to have
an eating party."

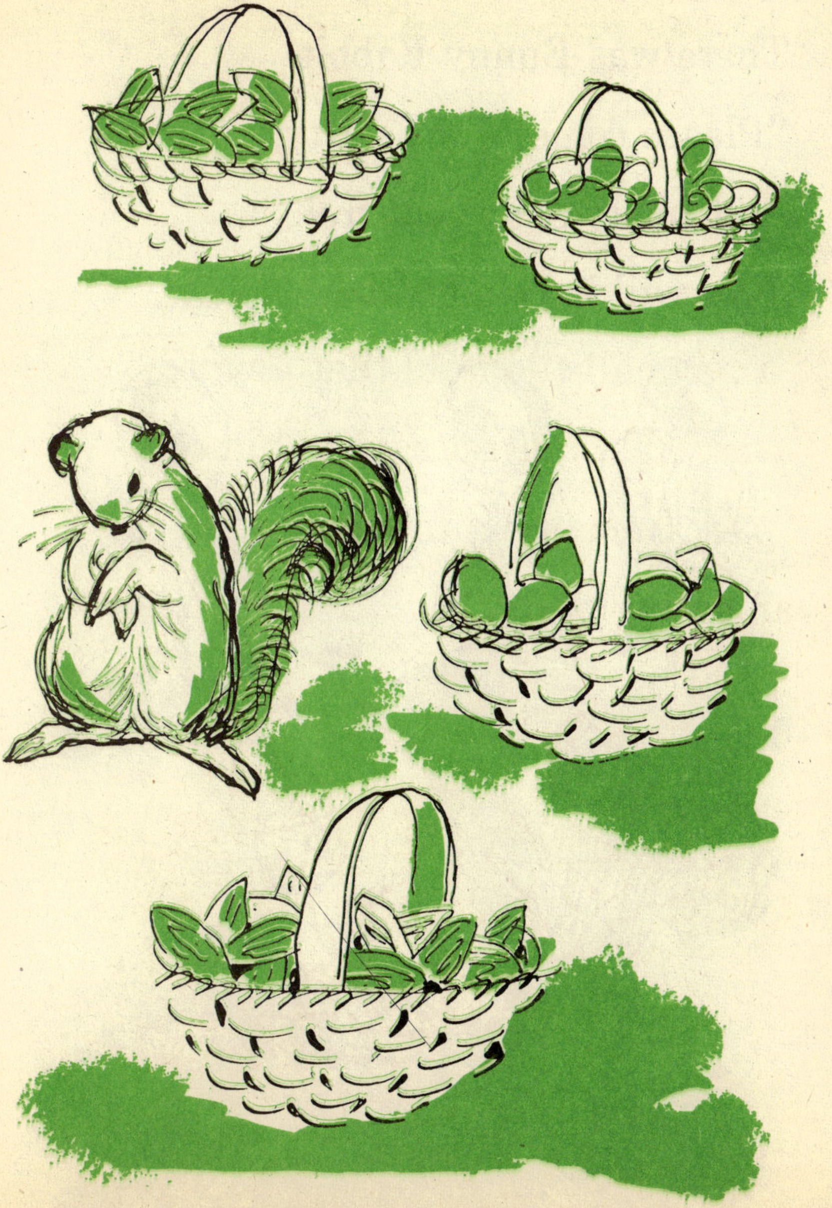

He ran back to the garden.

There was Bunny Rabbit.

"Please come to my party,"
said Little Gray Squirrel.

"We will have something to eat."

Bunny Rabbit looked very happy.
"Something good to eat?" he said.
"Oh, yes! I will come.
I love carrots!"

And away he went, hop-hop-hop,
to get ready for the party.

"Carrots?" said Squirrel to himself.
"I did not say anything
about carrots!"

Then he went to see
Old Brown Dog
to ask him to the party.
"Please come,"
said Little Gray Squirrel.
"We will have something
very good to eat."

"Something very good?"
said Old Brown Dog.
"That sounds just like bones.
Yes, I will come.
I love bones!"

And away he went to get ready
for the party.

"Bones!" said Squirrel to himself.
"I did not say anything about bones!
Oh, dear!"

Then he ran off to tell
Old White Cat.

"Do come to my party,"
said Little Gray Squirrel.
"We will have something good
to eat."
Old White Cat looked very happy.

"That must be fish," she said.
"Nothing is better than fish.
Thank you for asking me.
I will come."

And away she went to get ready for the party.

"Fish!" said Little Gray Squirrel to himself.

"I did not say anything about fish! Oh, my!"

He went off to look for Sparrow.

There was Sparrow still talking, talking, way up in the tree.
"Will you come to my party?" asked Little Gray Squirrel.
"We will have something good to eat."

Sparrow looked very happy.

"I know! I know!" he said.

"You are going to have seeds.

Seeds of the weed!

That's for me.

Oh, yes.

I will be there."

Squirrel looked up at Sparrow.

"Seeds!" he said to himself.

"I did not say anything
about seeds!"

Little Gray Squirrel sat down
under the tree.

He sat down to think.

Then he said to Sparrow,
"No! I cannot have a party
after all."
"What's this? What's this?"
said Sparrow.
"But I want to go
to an eating party."

So Little Gray Squirrel
told Sparrow everything.

"Carrots!" said Squirrel.

"That's what Bunny Rabbit wants.

Bones! That's what Old Dog wants.

Fish! That's what White Cat wants.

And seeds! That's what you want.

Seeds of the weed!

Whatever *they* are!"

Poor Squirrel!

He did not look very happy.

"And all I have," he said,

"are nuts to eat,

good brown nuts."

"I know!" said Sparrow. "I know!

I know how

you can have the party."

He told Squirrel what they could do.

And that was just what they did.

They all came to the eating party

at Little Gray Squirrel's house.

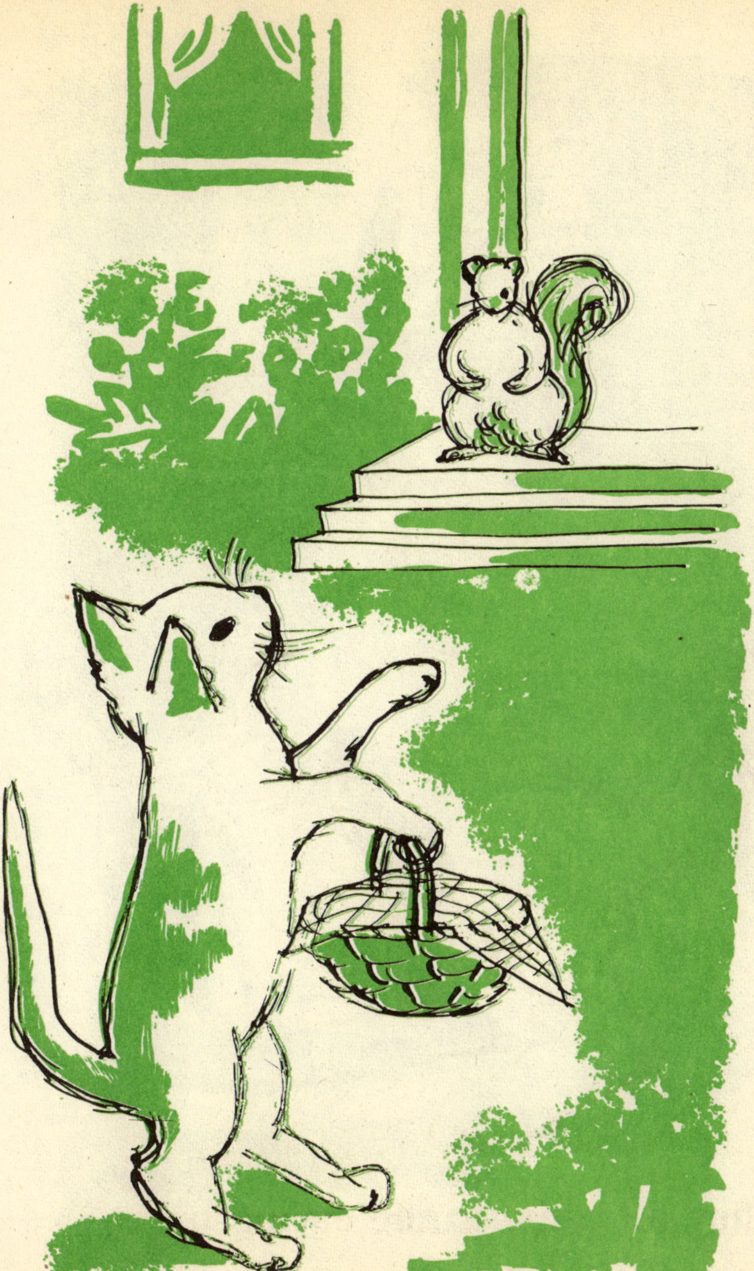

Bunny Rabbit came,

and he brought some carrots.

Old Brown Dog came,

and he brought some bones.

Old White Cat came,
and she brought some fish.

And Sparrow came
with many seeds.

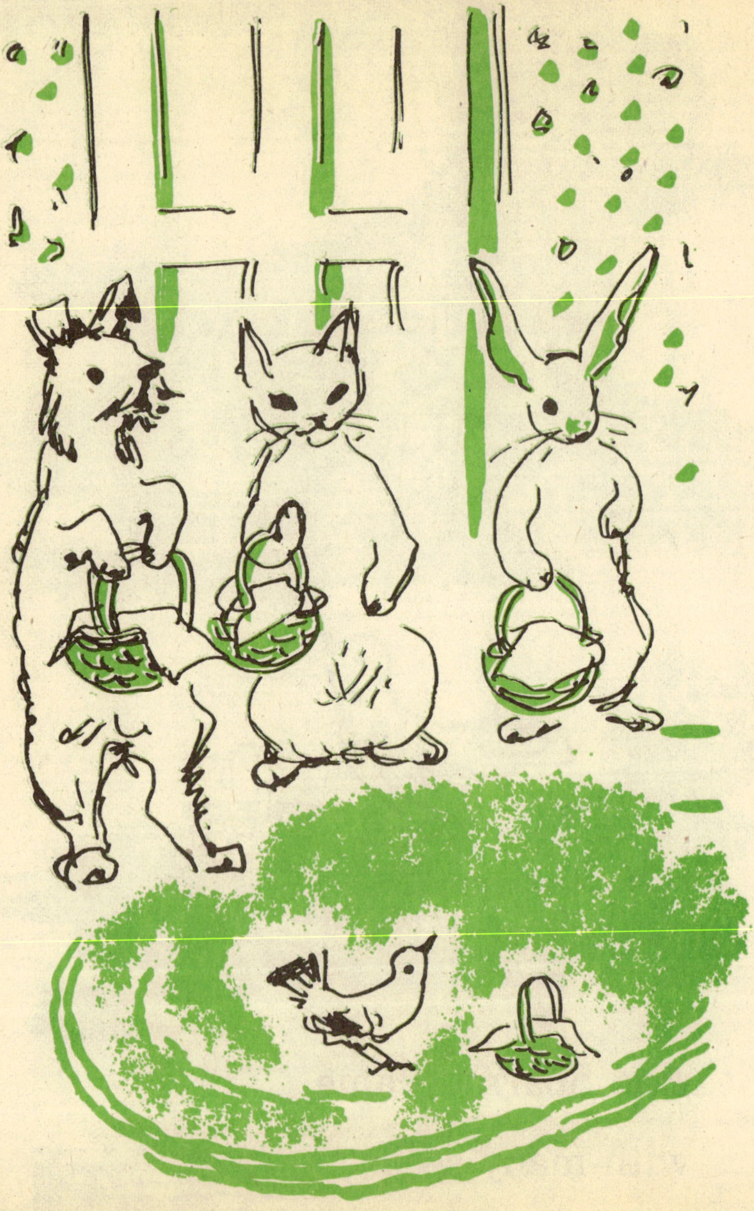

Little Gray Squirrel took out
the nuts he had put away.
Then they all sat down to eat.

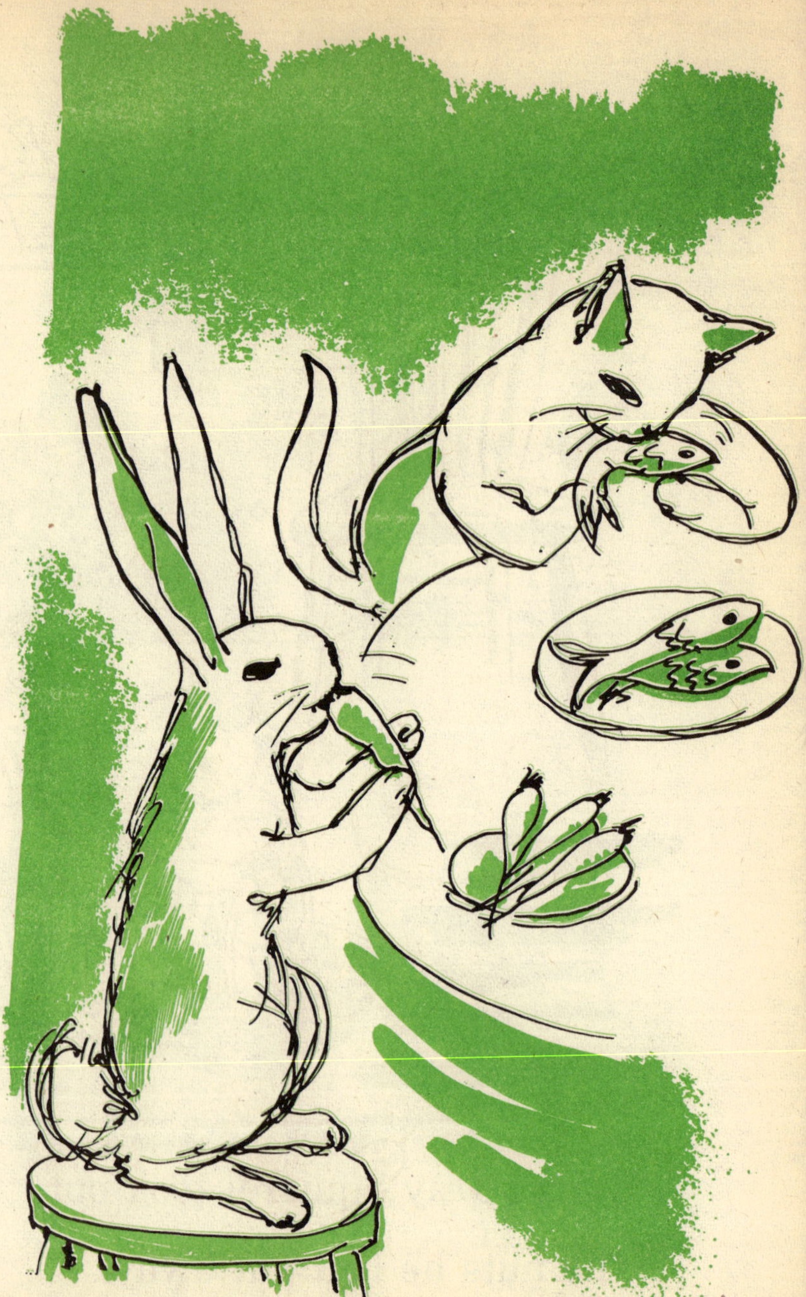

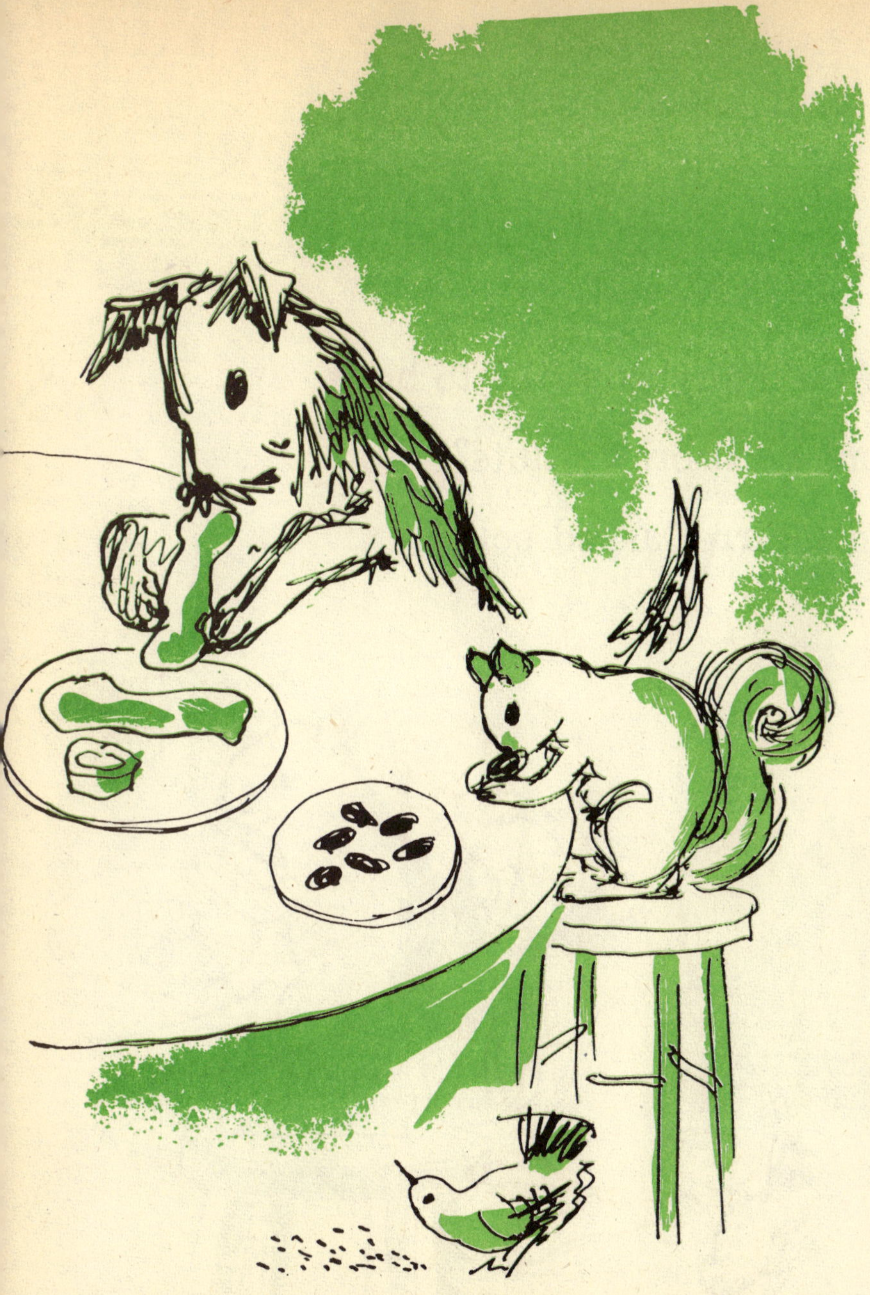

"Would anybody like to have
some good brown nuts?"
the squirrel asked politely.

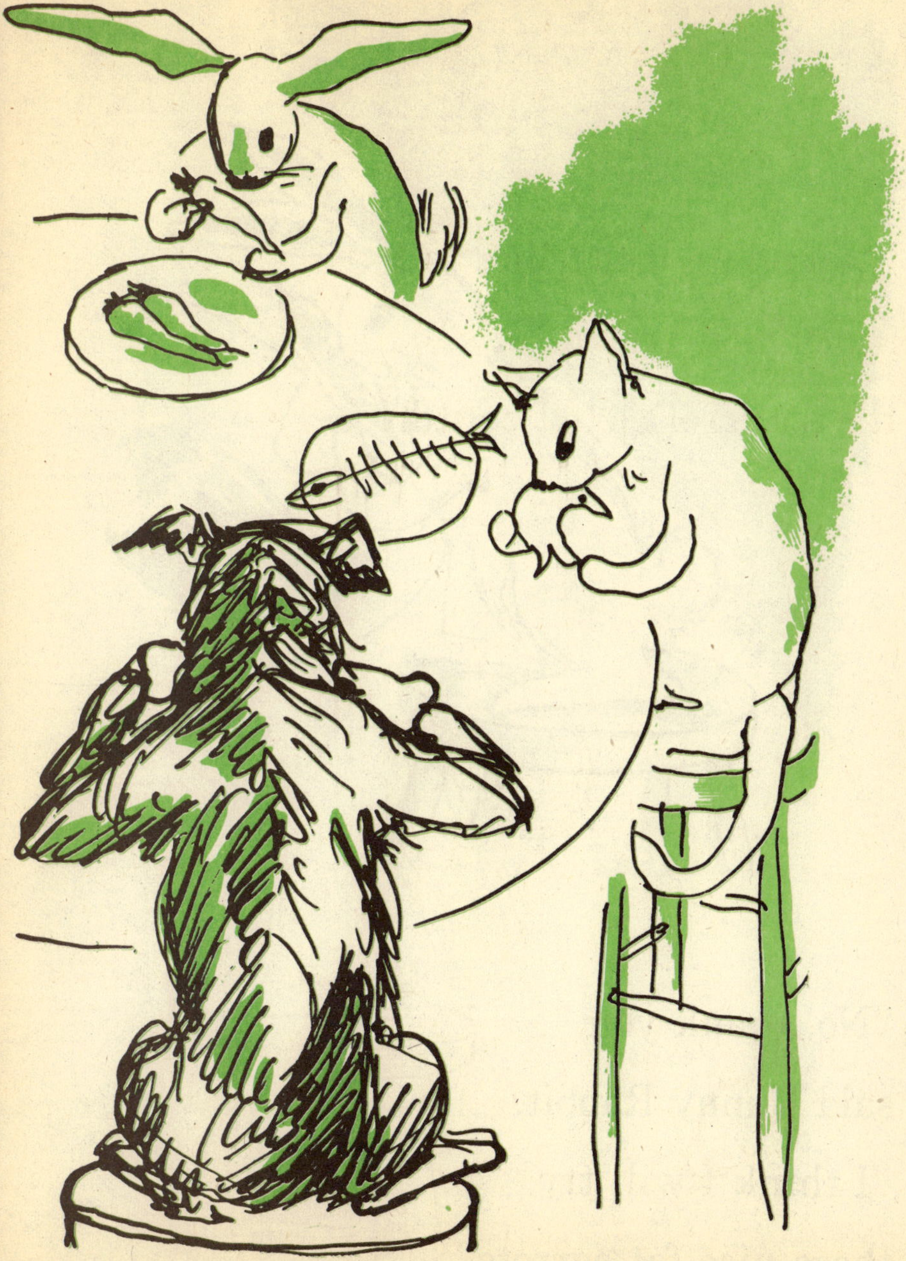

"No, thank you,"
said Bunny Rabbit.
"I think I will try
those nice fat carrots."

"No, thank you," said the cat.
"I will have
some of that good fish."

"No, thank you,"
said Old Brown Dog.
"Those bones do look so good."

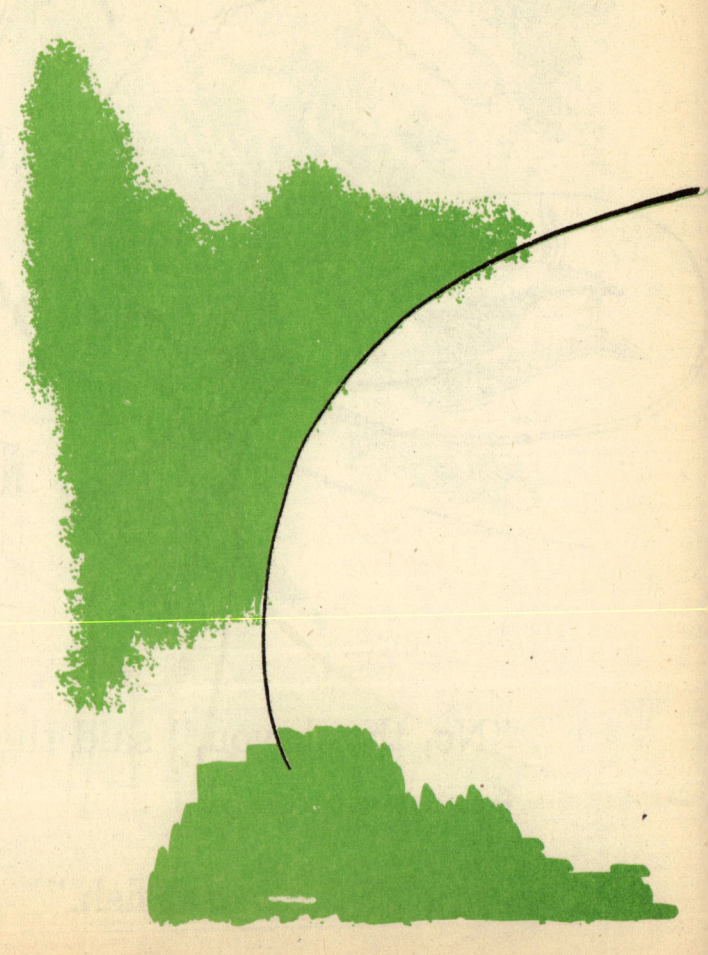

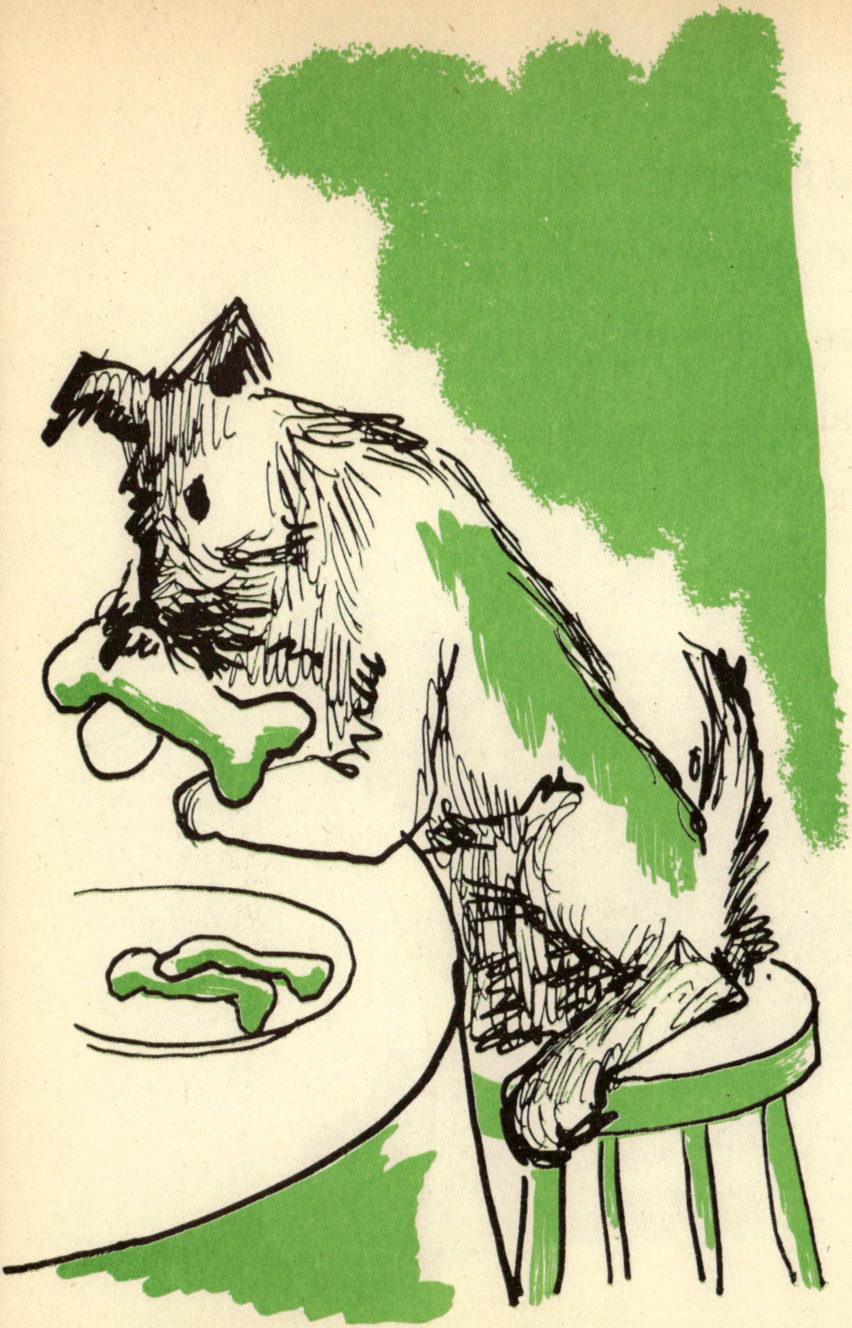

And Sparrow said,

"No, thank you, Squirrel.

I see some seeds.

That's what I like.

Seeds of the weed."

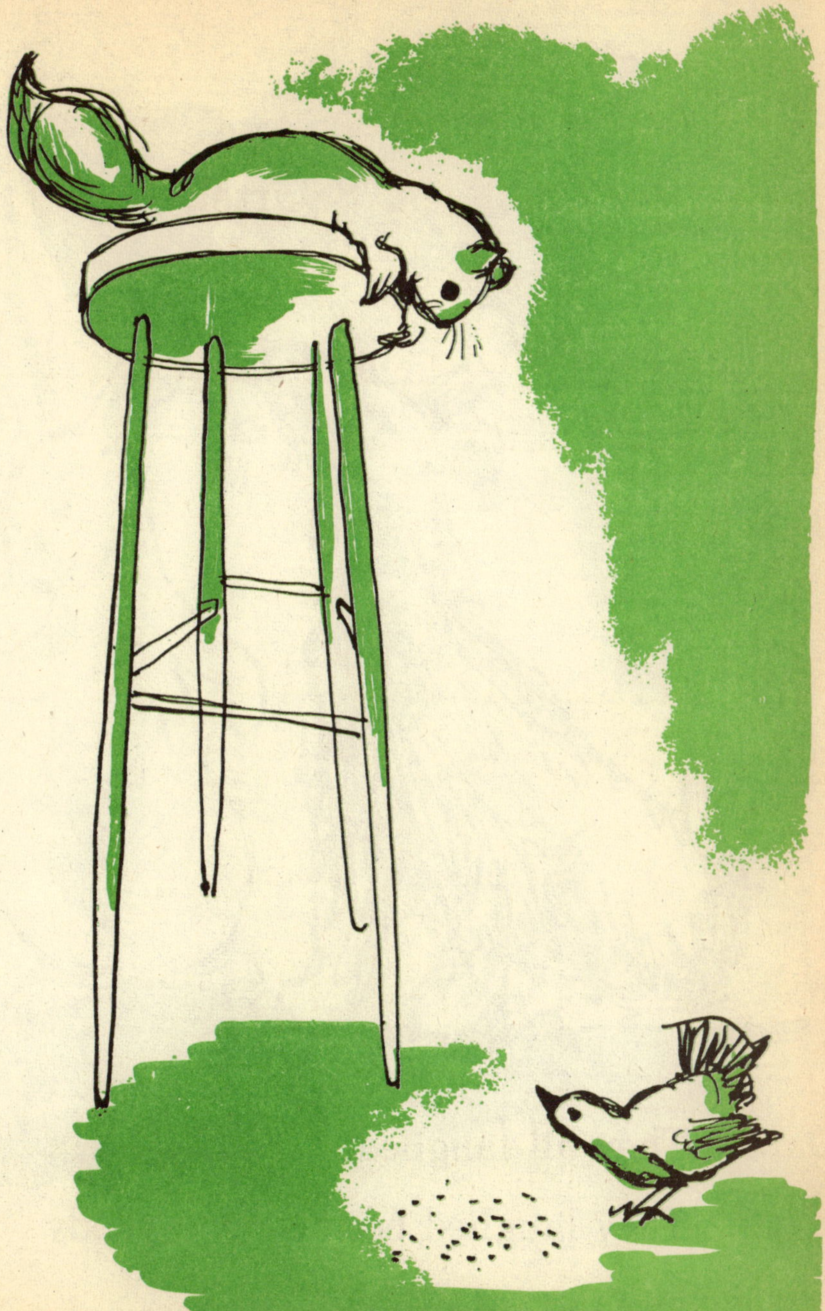

They all laughed.

They laughed because everybody had just what he wanted.

And they all said it was
the very best eating party
they ever had.

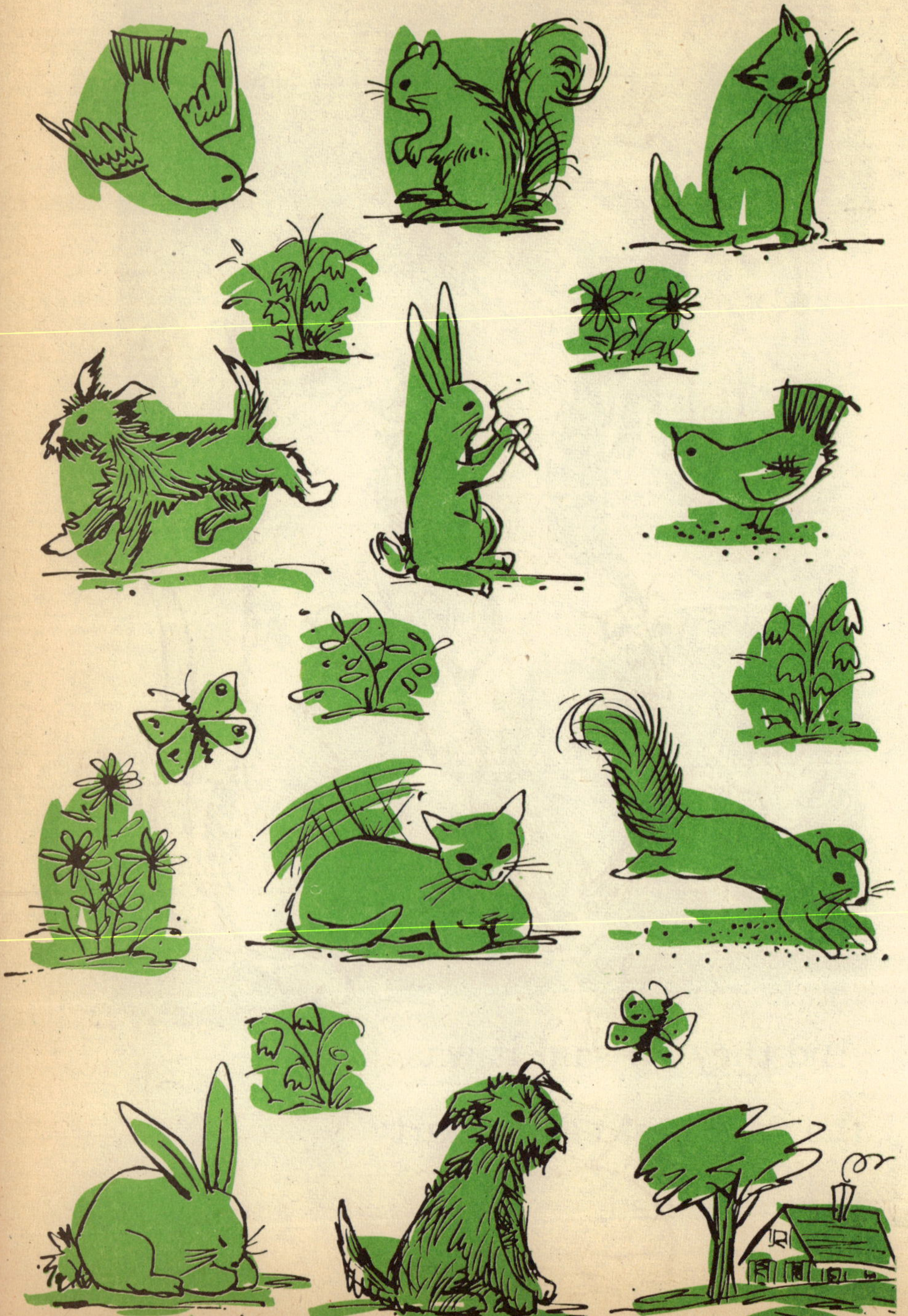

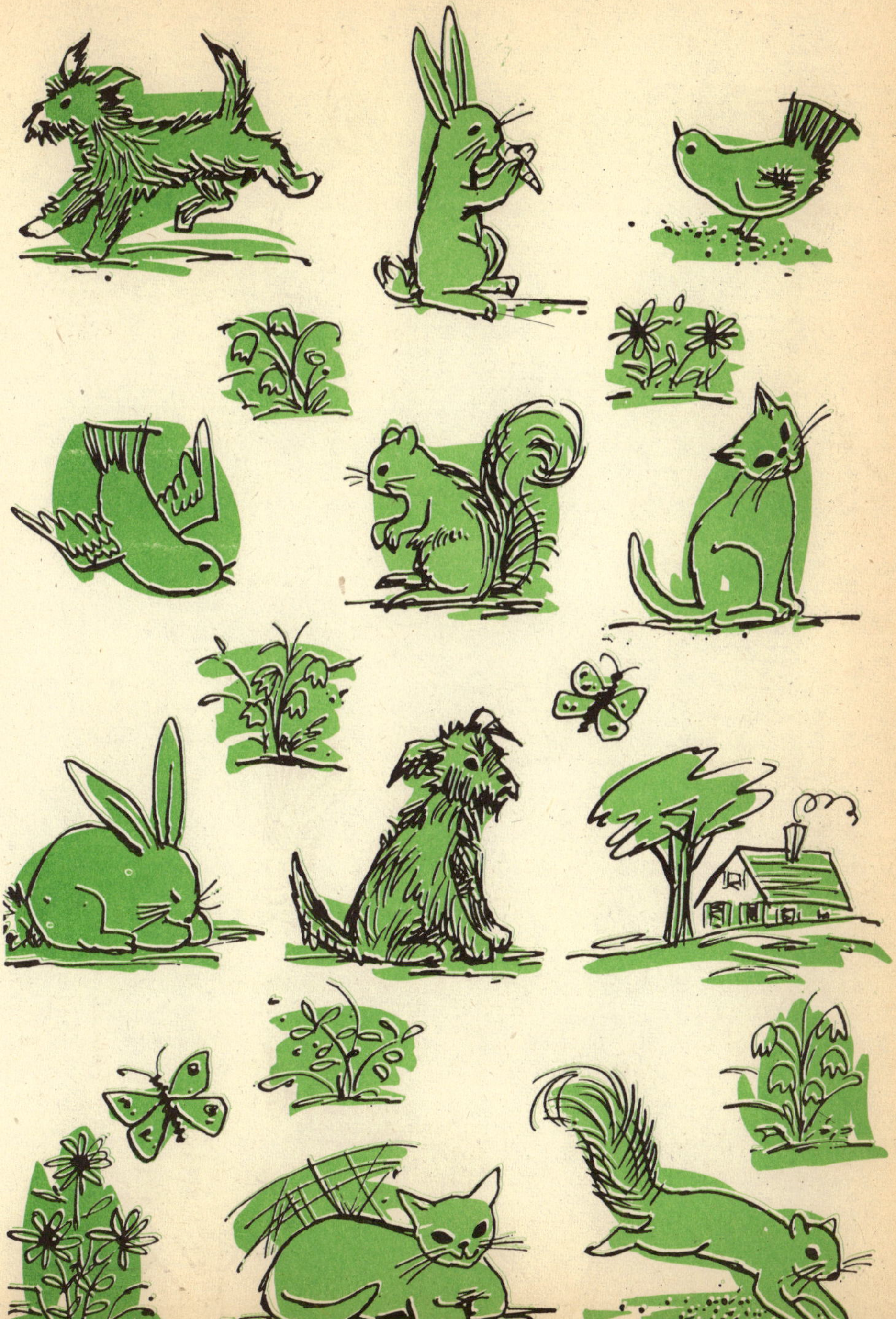

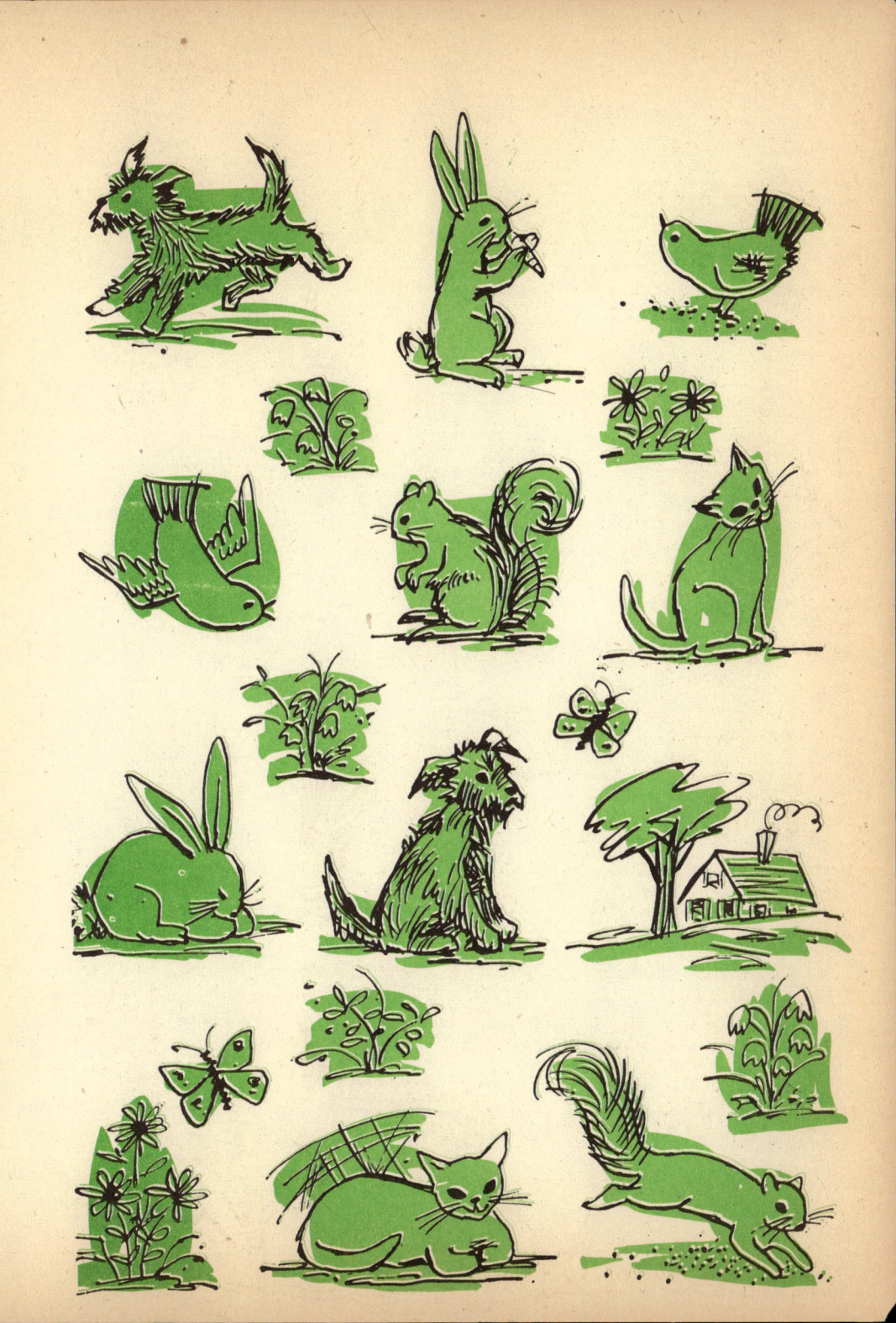